QUICK SKILLS

LISTENING
AND
OBSERVING

QUICK SKILLS

LISTENING
AND
OBSERVING

Judith D. Winzurk

Career Solutions Training Group
Paoli, PA

VISIT US ON THE INTERNET
school.cengage.com
academic.cengage.com

SOUTH-WESTERN
CENGAGE Learning

Australia • Brazil • Japan • Korea • Mexico • Singapore • Spain • United Kingdom • United States

Peter McBride: Business Unit Director
Eve Lewis: Team Leader
Laurie Wendell: Project Manager
Alan Biondi: Editor
Patricia Matthews Boies: Production Manager
Kathy Hampton: Manufacturing Coordinator
Mark Linton: Marketing Manager
Linda Wasserman: Marketing Coordinator

Thanks to the following educators and trainers
who provided valuable assistance during the development of the QUICK SKILLS materials:

Robert W. Moses
Vice President for Planning and Program Development
Indian River Community College
Fort Pierce, Florida

Richard Winn
Director, Educational Projects
Heald Colleges
San Francisco, California

Debra Mills
Education-to-Careers/Tech Prep Director
Danville Area Community College
Danville, Illinois

Patrick Highland
Director of Vocational Education
Iowa City Community School District
Iowa City, Iowa

Julie Kibler
Business Teacher and Business Department Chairperson
Castle High School
Newburgh, Indiana

Dave Hyslop
External Liaison
Bowling Green State University
Bowling Green, Ohio

Dr. Doris Humphrey: Project Manager
Jane Galli: Production Editor
Pam Dooley: Typography

13 East Central Avenue, Paoli, PA 19301
Telephone: 1-888-299-2784 • FAX: (610) 993-8249
E-mail: cstg@bellatlantic.net • Website: www.careersolutionsgroup.com

CONTENTS

Listening is an important part of everyday life, both at home and at work. Though students receive limited listening training in school, listening is the most used communication skill. Developing an awareness of the importance of listening can provide an advantage in your career.

Whether you are a salesman listening to a customer's needs, a supervisor listening to an employee's goals, a co-worker listening to casual conversation at the water cooler, a counselor listening to a patient, or a telemarketer conducting telephone sales calls, the more you listen, the more successful you will be in your work. Recognizing that listening is a skill you can develop starts you on the way to becoming a more effective communicator.

To get a head start on listening, it is important to evaluate your current listening skills. Answer each of the questions below, then make notes regarding which points you need the most help with. As you go through the workshops, pay particular attention to these points.

1. Hearing and listening are the same thing.

2. Smart listeners use all of their senses.

3. Most people listen to 50 percent of what is being said.

4. Good listeners interrupt the speaker with questions and comments.

5. Different situations require different kinds of listening.

6. Both internal and external barriers affect listening.

7. Great listeners have learned to ignore non-verbal communications.

8. We all listen with the same set of listening filters.

9. Identifying listening filters will help you become a better listener.

10. Great listeners make better employees.

Answers: F, T, F, T, T, F, T, F, T, T

How did you do on your self-assessment? If you gave a few wrong answers, don't worry; the upcoming workshops will help you become a better listener.

When you find yourself in the role of listener, several strategies can help you become more effective. You'll learn about these strategies as you study the workshops in this Quick Skills book. In Workshop 1, you will learn to analyze your listening habits and become a better listener. Workshop 2 introduces the reasons and ways people listen and is followed by Workshop 3 which focuses on internal and external listening. In Workshop 4, you will learn about the role of non-verbal communication in listening; and in Workshop 5, you will identify listening filters that interfere with messages between speaker and listener. Workshop 6 tells you how to become a better listener, and Workshop 7 describes how you can get others to listen to you. Telephone listening skills are covered in Workshop 8.

Jordan sits staring at the seminar speaker, lost in her thoughts. She was invited to this seminar about computers because a position she's interested in has opened up and one of the requirements is to be knowledgable about her company's computer system.

She is having a hard time with the technical discussion, so her mind begins to wander. She has several questions to ask and interrupted once, but the seminar leader asked her to hold her questions until the end.

She makes a mental list of all the work waiting on her desk—a report to be typed, a presentation to prepare, and an unhappy customer to call. She is stressed just being at the seminar because it takes time that she would prefer to devote to her daily tasks.

She starts to think about everything she has to do at home— call a caterer about her wedding reception, find a place to board her cat during the honeymoon, and sublet her apartment. She tries to concentrate, but finds it hard to do.

Now and then she shifts in her seat, just in case anyone thinks she isn't listening. In fact, she can repeat the speaker's last several words. But is she listening?

> Listening well is as powerful a means of communication and influence as talking well.
>
> — John Marshall

What's Inside

In these pages, you will learn to:

Listening Is More Than Hearing

Even though you hear, you may not be listening. Sure, you're picking up the sounds all around you-music, voices, background noises. But are you tuned in?

Hearing is one of the five senses, and unless a person is hearing impaired, hearing occurs naturally. To hear, you don't have to concentrate—the sounds are just present. But listening is learned, and it's harder. With listening comes the need to sense, interpret, and evaluate what you hear.

Has anyone ever made the comments that are shown in the box to you?

"You never listen to me."
"Didn't you hear what I said?"
"How many times do I have to tell you?"
"If I've told you once, I've told you a thousand times."
"Pay attention."
"Look at me when I talk."
"Put your antennae up."

Use All Your Senses to Listen

Think of the last conversation you had today. Did you use only your ears? Or did you watch the speaker's face for clues to what was being said, allowing your eyes to help you listen?

When you are at lunch and a friend says, "They're serving pizza today," does your sense of smell confirm the message? And after the first bite, does your sense of taste give feedback that you heard the right message, telling you, "Yes, this is pizza."

If someone says, "I love you," does the warm hug—the sense of touch—help you understand the message. Smart workers put all five senses to work when they listen. While hearing is the motor that runs the listening engine, the senses are the supporting parts.

> If no one is listening and a tree falls in the forest, does the tree make a noise?
>
> — Anonymous

What do you hear?

Go silent and listen to the sounds around you that you usually ignore. Do you hear a computer humming, someone flipping pages at the desk next to you, or cars roaring or accelerating on the street outside?

Make a list of the sounds you hear.

_____

_____

_____

_____

_____

_____

_____

_____

_____

_____

_____

_____

_____

_____

_____

_____

_____

_____

_____

The Role of Listening

Forty percent of our communication time each day is spent listening, more than any other form of communication. In fact, business executives spend between 40 and 80 percent of their working hours listening to their superiors, subordinates, customers, vendors, and others. It is a big surprise, therefore, that we spend so little time preparing to be good listeners.

In 12 years of education, according to Madelyn Burley-Allen in her study of listening reported in *Listening: The Forgotten Skill*, no more than six months' time is devoted to listening training. Speaking, on the other hand, receives 1-2 years of training, while reading receives 6-8 years and writing receives 12 years. Think back to your listening education before this course. Had you ever before had a course in listening? Or a unit on listening?

Listening is a process that begins with a speaker, travels to a receiver of the message, often returns to the speaker in the form of a question or a response from the receiver, and is recycled by the speaker to the listener. This pattern may be repeated several times and is called feedback.

The message often gets confused, and the listener doesn't receive the same message the speaker meant to send. That's because individuals interpret information differently, depending on age, gender, ethnic group, education, economic status, religious background, and other characteristics. For example, adults and teenagers often disagree about what they hear in song lyrics because of their different emotions and backgrounds.

Feedback

Speaking ← → **Listening**

Feedback

Further complicating a person's ability to be a good listener is the mismatch between speaking speed and thinking speed. Since the human brain processes information at more than 400 words a minute and the average speaker talks at the rate of only 125-150 words a minute, the mind has time to idle. Not liking this, it keeps busy by shuffling through a variety of thoughts, losing the speaker's words in the process. You'll learn more about listening as you continue the workshops, but for now, just remember that listening isn't simple.

Listening for different purposes

Several different types of workers are listed below. For each one, write why listening is important in the person's job. At the end of the exercise, name three other workers whose jobs require good listening skills and explain why.

Nurse _____

School bus driver _____

Lawyer _____

Actor _____

Newspaper reporter _____

Highway patrol officer _____

Scientist _____

Airplane pilot _____

Advertising copywriter _____

Hotel desk clerk _____

Truck driver _____

Salesperson _____

_____ _____

_____ _____

_____ _____

> " It is the province of knowledge to speak and
> it is the privilege of wisdom to listen. "
>
> — Oliver Wendell Holmes

Listening to One of Four Words

Do you daydream, plan what you want to say next, or stop listening altogether because you assume you know what the speaker is going to say? Or do you interrupt, talk while others are talking, and wait for conversations to slow so you can jump in? If you are like most people, characteristics like these cause you to listen carefully only about 25 percent of the time. Is it any wonder, then, that individuals misunderstand, fail to follow directions, and make mistakes in their work and personal lives?

The reasons people don't listen are many and varied, but some of the more common reasons are discussed below. As you read, ask yourself if you're guilty of any of these listening habits.

Daydreaming.

Taking mental vacations is relaxing, especially when a speaker drones on and on; but this practice can be dangerous if the speaker is your supervisor, a customer, a co-worker on your project, or another person who is instrumental to your career success. If you take a daydreaming break just when a question is asked, expect to be embarrassed and prepare to stumble through an apology.

When you find your mind drifting, sit up straight, look the speaker in the eye, ask questions, and join in the conversation.

Racing ahead.

Bright thinkers often race ahead in their thoughts, so they fail to listen carefully to the speaker. Take Michael for example. This bright, young architect almost lost a potential customer during their first meeting. As the client described his project, Michael became so excited that he started thinking about a possible design. Because he had not been listening, he suggested a plan the customer had just said was out of the question. Although Michael's enthusiasm for his work is admirable, the best way he can help his customers is to listen to them.

You, also, may need to put the brakes on your creative process and return your concentration to the speaker when your enthusiasm interferes with effective listening.

> " Nothing is quite so annoying as to have someone go right on talking when you keep interrupting. "
>
> — Unknown

May I interrupt? If questions pop into your head as you listen to a speaker, you may tend to ask them as they occur. Interrupting a speaker with questions, comments, or other side notes may derail conversations altogether, distracting everyone involved in the conversation. At the minimum, interrupting a speaker is rude.

Hold your questions and comments until the speaker has finished or comes to a point in the conversation where input is invited.

Talking instead of listening. You know your ideas are good, and you want to communicate them. Maybe you find it hard to listen because you're waiting for a chance to talk. If you are planning what to say when it is your turn, then you aren't really listening to the speaker.

Putting words in their mouth. You know where the conversation is heading. Before a speaker can get the words out, you jump in with what you think is about to be said.

Jumping ahead in the conversation and second-guessing means you aren't concentrating on being a listener; instead, you are preparing to be the speaker.

Consider the auto mechanic who suggests a variety of repairs for a customer's car while the customer tries to explain the problem. Is the mechanic listening? Do you think the customer will be offended by this rudeness?

> " The older I get the more I listen to people who don't talk much. "
>
> — German G. Glien

Case Study.

Suzanne, Juan, and Amelia, laboratory technicians at a geriatric center, are participating in team training on fire evacuation procedures for their elderly patients. As the team leader describes which patients will use each hallway in case of an emergency, Juan thinks about the extra money he will get from his raise next week. Suzanne, meanwhile, jumps in and asks a question. Amelia, who considers herself an excellent employee because she loves her work, is waiting for a chance to explain her better idea about evacuations.

What listening mistake is each of the employees making? What consequences could result from the mistakes?

Juan's mistake _____

Potential consequences _____

_____

_____

Suzanne's mistake _____

Potential consequences _____

_____

_____

Amelia's mistake _____

Potential consequences _____

_____

_____

> " No one ever listened
> themselves out of a job. "
>
> — Calvin Coolidge

Five ways to become a better listener

Would you like to spend more time problem solving and less time correcting errors? If this question gets an easy yes, then you can start by becoming a better listener. Use the five tested methods described below to eliminate misunderstandings, misinformation, and wasted time.

1. **Make eye contact with the speaker.** Watch a speaker's face for clues to the message, because facial expressions often give away secrets. "No" accompanied by a smile carries a different message than "no" accompanied by a frown and a stern stare.

2. **Concentrate on what the speaker is saying.** Be attentive and interested in what speakers say. Try to put yourself in their shoes, attempting to see things from their point of view. Show speakers that you are following a conversation as it progresses by saying things like "yes, I see" and "oh, really." Basically your job is to concentrate on concentrating.

3. **Tune out distractions.** Give speakers your undivided attention. Don't answer the phone, continue working on the computer, glance at your watch, or look around the room or office when someone is speaking with you. Block out mannerisms and behaviors that distract you. Focus on what is being said.

4. **Ask questions for clarity.** Don't assume anything. If you don't understand the speaker or information is unclear, ask questions. Start your questions with the following phrases:
"Do you mean .... "
"Are you saying that ..."
"Do I understand that what you are saying is ..."
"I think you are saying ..."
The timing for asking questions is very important. Don't ask questions during the flow of the conversation. Instead, hold them until an appropriate time, typically toward the conclusion of the speaker's message.

5. **Rephrase the speaker's comments.** Confirm what you heard by restating what the speaker said. Rephrase comments or statements made by the speaker, or summarize the message you think you just heard. This provides the speaker with an opportunity to correct any misunderstandings or misinterpretations immediately.

Analyze Your Listening Habits

Do you listen attentively in some situations and inattentively in others? Do you detect a pattern to your listening behavior? Take some time now to think about all the listening you've done today. In column 1, write the name of several people to whom you have listened; in column 2, write the subject of the conversation; in column 3, write attentive or inattentive to describe your listening behavior. Analyze why you were more attentive some times than others, then write five words to describe the attentive situations.

Name of speaker	Subject	Attentive/Inattentive	Reason for behavior
Zachary Adams	Computer repair	Attentive	My computer was broken

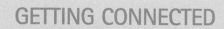

GETTING CONNECTED

For additional information on improving your listening skills, log on to the Internet and visit the Web site *LAL - Sharpen Your Listening Skills at*

http://www.mc3.edu/peopplac/lib/lal/workshops/listeningskills.html

WORKSHOP WRAP-UP

- Listening requires concentration because we think faster than we talk.
- Hearing is a sense most people are born with, but listening is a skill that must be learned.
- Reasons why people don't listen are daydreaming, racing ahead of the speaker, interrupting, waiting for a chance to talk, and putting words in the speaker's mouth.
- Five ways to become a better listener are: making eye contact with the speaker, concentrating on what is being said, tuning out distractions, asking questions for clarity, and rephrasing what's been said.

2 WORKSHOP

"But Grant, that's not what I thought you said." Ann takes a deep breath and realizes she has made a huge mistake.

Grant stands frowning at a packing slip for 10,000 copies of the newsletter just delivered to his office. "I said only the top accounts were to receive the newsletter," he tells her sharply. "You should have ordered only a thousand copies."

During the staff meeting last week, she thought she heard Grant say that all customers were to receive a copy of the company's first newsletter. That day, the meeting was running long and she was thinking about what she wanted to wear to Malin's party this weekend.

She had been only half listening, and now she feels guilty. She knows she has a tendency to let her mind wander during meetings, and it has gotten her into some embarrassing situations before, but nothing like this.

Ann's heart sinks as Grant hands her the packing slip. She is responsible for this costly error to the company. She wonders how it will affect her annual review which Grant will conduct in about six weeks.

What's Inside

In these pages, you will learn to:

> Let others confide in you. It may not help you, but it will help them.
>
> — Roger G. Imhoff

Reasons for Listening

People listen for many reasons. The more important the reason, the more attention listeners pay to the speaker. For example, you may find yourself listening intently when your supervisor discusses promotions or raises or when your instructor gives directions about an upcoming test. You listen less intently when you are in the middle of a project and a co-worker mentions an upcoming schedule change. Here are several reasons for listening.

Personal Involvement

Having a stake or personal involvement in a subject helps people concentrate on what a speaker says. For example, if your supervisor calls you to his office to discuss a job you did well or poorly, your antennae will tune the message in more quickly than if the same supervisor explains a technical topic that does not relate to your daily tasks.

To Get Information

Most of a listener's time is for the purpose of getting information or instructions. Your supervisors, coworkers and customers dispense a great deal of verbal information daily. If you are not engaged in what they have to say, you may be unable to perform your job satisfactorily.

To Learn Something New

Each day offers many opportunities to learn something new and different. New information presents a special challenge to the listener because it must be related to other things you know. For example, when you are presented with information that connects loosely to your work, sort through what you hear and decide which details are relevant to both your job and the company's big picture or bottom line. Those are the details that matter to you personally.

To Show Concern

Listening with empathy, showing concern, offering support, helping others explore options, or simply being a soundboard for people trying to make difficult decisions are powerful reasons for listening. Sometimes the best solution you can offer during a crisis simply is to listen.

> " So when you listen to somebody, completely, attentively, then you listen not only to the words, but also to the feeling of what is being conveyed, to the whole of it, not part of it. "
>
> — Jiddu Krishnamurti

To build relationships

Building professional and personal connections is key to your career success. Whether you are listening to a co-worker with a problem, a team member's idea or a colleague's description of a weekend adventure—each of these represents an opportunity to strengthen a relationship. These are times when you should remain silent and allow others to talk. Adding a few good questions and positive feedback will keep the conversation moving, and the other person will think, "What a good conversationalist!"

When a penalty is apparent

The intensity with which you listen may depend on the consequences associated with *not listening*. Most people become better listeners when the stakes for *not* listening are higher than the stakes for listening. The degree to which you listen or the amount of concentration required depends on the situation. If you are listening to casual conversations among friends, you concentrate less than if you are receiving instructions from a physician on how to cure a medical problem.

As a courtesy

Some listening falls into the category of good manners or courtesy. For example, relaying messages between two people who can't speak personally, listening to a story about a co-worker's new dog, or allowing a supervisor to repeat an instruction he has already given several times are examples of courteous listening.

Reasons for Listening

- Personal Involvement
- To Get Information
- To Learn Something New
- To Show Concern
- To Build Relationships
- When a Penalty Is Apparent
- As a Courtesy

Why Listen?

Why we listen has a lot to do with how we listen. Apply the reasons for listening to each situation in the list below. Give three reasons why each person should listen.

Your automobile insurance agent calls you at home with information regarding new insurance coverage for your car.

1._____

2._____

3._____

Your supervisor holds a mandatory meeting for all staff about the upcoming restructuring of jobs.

1._____

2._____

3._____

An unhappy customer calls you about the performance of a power tool she purchased for a friend for his birthday.

1._____

2._____

3._____

You answer the telephone and take a message for a colleague.

1._____

2._____

3._____

The Ways We Listen

Different situations require different types of listening, so you spend your days listening intently to some speakers and casually to others. This works just fine until you slip up and listen casually when you should be listening intently. Four ways to listen are described in the chart below. While it is not necessary always to identify which way you are listening, it's good to know the difference.

Four Ways to Listen

Methods of Listening	Explanation and Examples
Empathetic listening	Listening for understanding *Listening to friends about their personal concerns* *Listening to opposing opinions*
Critical listening	Listening for information *Listening to directions* *Listening to instructions from teachers or supervisors*
Appreciative listening	Listening for enjoyment *Listening to a play, concert, radio, television or a video*
Selective listening	Listening in spurts. *Tuning in and out of the conversations* *Waiting for a chance to talk* *Thinking of your response while the speaker talks*

> " Listen. Don't explain or justify. "
>
> — Wilheim G. Ryer

How I Listened Today

Think about today and list specific situations in which you used each listening method described earlier. Write a few words to describe how you could have improved your listening in each case, then analyze the chart to determine whether you have a listening pattern. Make three recommendations for how you can be a better listener.

	Person Speaking	Subject	Type of Listening I Did
Empathetic listening	_____	_____	_____
	_____	_____	_____
Critical listening	_____	_____	_____
	_____	_____	_____
Appreciative listening	_____	_____	_____
	_____	_____	_____
Selective listening	_____	_____	_____
	_____	_____	_____

My primary listening method: _____

Ways I can become a better listener: _____

_____

_____

_____

_____

_____

_____

_____

_____

_____

_____

_____

Active Listening Strategies

Are you an active or passive listener? An active listener engages in empathetic, critical, and appreciative listening. This person concentrates on the main ideas, acknowledges understanding through feedback, and refrains from evaluation or judgment of the speaker.

The least effective listener is the passive listener, one who listens selectively or in spurts. These individuals receive only half the message or misinterpret or misunderstand the intended message because they do not pay attention.

Ten strategies for active listening are discussed below.

Concentrate

If you are supposed to be listening, then listen. Don't think about the pile of work on your desk, how you are going to spend your holiday next week, or what's waiting at home. If you listen with one ear instead of two, you may miss half the conversation—perhaps the most important half.

Listen for key words

Although understanding the overall message is the ultimate goal of a conversation, a listener should be alert to key words or phrases as the speaker talks. Listen for some of these: "Let me emphasize..." or "I want to make this very clear to everyone ...", or "special attention should be given to the information that follows."

Listen to content

Active listeners focus on the content of a message. This requires the ability to discriminate between facts, assumptions, biases, and opinions voiced by the speaker. With critical listening skills, you are able to sift through the information that is irrelevant and capture the crucial elements of a conversation, a speech, or a lecture. A co-worker who wishes you to support his idea for a new procedure will try to convince you of its value. As a listener, you must be able to separate the content from the speaker's enthusiasm.

> " Nature gave us one tongue and two ears so we could hear twice as much as we speak. "
>
> — Epictetus

Refrain from Judging

An arrogant, opinionated, or boastful speaker is hard to enjoy, but such a person may have valuable information. Other important speakers may be timid, use bad grammar, or work in a lower-level position than yours. Don't judge their message by factors unrelated to what they have to say, or you lose an important opportunity for knowledge they can pass along.

Listen to Intensity

Intensity is an umbrella term that refers to the volume and tone of a speaker's voice, the speed of delivery, and the emotion with which the words are spoken. If a speaker's voice is tense, sharp, nervous, or unfriendly, an active listener picks up the clues right away and knows that they signify stress, frustration, anger, or fear. Positive clues, such as pleasure, excitement, and sincerity, are also clear to the practiced listener.

A copy machine service technician jokingly says she listens for the hysteria in her clients' voices before deciding her priority assignments for the day. While no management expert would recommend this method of prioritizing, this savvy listener knows to listen to voice intensity when deciding which repairs are emergencies and which are routine.

Listen for Mood

"You did a great job," spoken with a smile, a handshake, or a confirming, positive nod means something different from the same words spoken with sarcasm or a frown. The mood and demeanor of the speaker communicates as much, and often more than, the words. Consider the posture, facial expressions, gestures, and other body language displayed by your manager during your yearly review. Did she seem relaxed and unhurried? Did she smile and make eye contact as she discussed your work habits? Or did she sit tall and stiff in her chair and look down at her desk during the meeting? Regardless of how she behaved, she was providing clues to her the mood. Non-verbal behavior and its relationship to listening will be explored further in Workshop 4.

Listen with all the senses

From Workshop 1 you will remember that all five senses can aid listening. Your eyes observe and help you interpret body language; and the senses of smell and taste confirm messages about food, scents, and odors, while the sense of touch communicates friendship, concern, and camaraderie.

If a co-worker in a restaurant, for example, comes running to you with a bleeding hand, your eyes confirm an emergency as much as his actual words, "I cut myself." Being able to listen with all your senses is a key component of active listening.

Refrain from fixing

You may be a Mr. or Ms. FixIt, but fixing is not always what a listener wants. Sometimes you just need to listen, to let the speaker worry or vent in your presence. Children who accuse their parents of "always telling me what to do when I talk to them" most likely are saying, "I just want to talk. I don't want you to try to fix my problem." In your job, you will run into people who just want to talk, who don't want you to try to fix their problem. Stay silent. Let them talk.

Ask questions

Clarify messages that are unclear by asking additional questions or requesting the speaker to repeat the comment. If that doesn't work, restate the speaker's remarks in your own words and ask for verification that you are correct.

If you want additional information from the speaker, ask questions that require more in-depth answers, such as "When you first became aware that the company's profitability was in danger, what steps did you take that could help me as a small business owner?"

Give feedback

Speakers need to know what you are thinking so that they can take their remarks to the next level or address concerns they may have overlooked. As a speaker talks, use non-verbal language, such as nods of yes or no, facial puzzlement, or hand movements that suggest stop or wait a minute.

The Listeners I Know

Who is the best listener you know? Who is the worst? In the space below, describe the listening skills these individuals display that caused you to place them in these categories. Compare their listening skills to your own. Do your skills match those of the best listener or the worst listener?

The best listener I know

_____

_____

_____

Listening skills displayed by this person

_____

_____

_____

The worst listener I know

_____

_____

_____

Listening skills displayed by this person

_____

_____

_____

The listening characteristics I share:

With the best listener

_____

_____

_____

With the worst listener

_____

_____

_____

Rewards of Good Listening

People feel good when others listen to them. Information gets reported accurately, more work gets done, co-workers trust each other, and teams interact more effectively. If listening is not one of your strong points, it is time to develop the skill. You will probably find yourself in the majority because most people are not good listeners. This new work skill will take you beyond the ordinary ways that most people communicate in their day-to-day work.

Listening at Work

The consequences of not listening are mistakes, potential danger, frustration, and assorted other negatives. What would happen if the people below were not listening?

An airline pilot who gets instructions from an air traffic controller

_____

_____

A radiology lab assistant who receives directions from the doctor on tests to be ordered for a patient

_____

_____

A travel agent who plans a conference for an international company

_____

_____

A florist who takes an order from a customer

_____

_____

A physical therapist who gets feedback from a patient in pain

_____

_____

A school counselor in a conference with parents

_____

_____

A child care provider receiving instructions from a parent

_____

_____

A newspaper reporter interviewing a witness to an accident

_____

_____

GETTING CONNECTED

Log on to the Website below to get more information on listening skills needed for increased sales.

http://salesdoctors.com/diagnosis/3listen.htm

WORKSHOP WRAP-UP

- People listen for different reasons depending upon the situation.
- The four main ways of listening are empathetic, critical, appreciative, and selective.
- Active listening involves concentrating on the speaker's words, content, intensity, and mood.
- Anyone can be a good listener by devoting time and energy.

3 WORKSHOP

Luis glances at his watch as his client talks on and on about the specifications for a Website he wants Luis to design. For a while Luis concentrates, but his mind drifts away. He has heard the same instructions half a dozen times over the last few weeks. He wants to get started, but his client demands meeting after meeting to review the details.

Pretending to be listening but thinking about other things, Luis wonders, "Is it time for lunch yet? I have some errands to run." He hears people in the hallway talking about a power walk in the park. He glances toward the door to see who is talking. He would really like to join the group; they take a walk together every day, and he picks up valuable information about what is going on in the company.

His attention returns to his client who is asking a question. "Will you repeat that?" Luis asks. His client seems surprised but rephrases her question. Luis can tell by her demeanor and the stiff look on her face that he has offended her. He spends the next several minutes trying to restore her confidence in him.

After the two finish their meeting and shake hands, a chill remains. Luis is disturbed by the crack in their former good relationship.

What's Inside

In these pages, you will learn to:

> " Let others confide in you. It may not help you, but it will help them. "
>
> — Roger G. Imhoff

Listening Interference

Loud noises, poor lighting in the room, the speaker's unusual attire, interruptions, people talking in the background, and other distractions create listening interference that is similar to radio static. This interference causes incorrect messages, confused instructions, misinterpretations of what is being said, delayed projects and hurt feelings.

If you were listening to the radio and encountered static, would you continue to listen? Probably not. Neither should you allow listening static to interfere with your communications.

Listening interference is costly to businesses. When static interferes with listening, it translates into lost time, money, and miss opportunity.

Four steps will help you eliminate or reduce listening interference:

Results of Listening Interference

· ·

✓ misunderstanding
✓ wasted time
✓ frustration
✓ hurt feelings

✓ confusion
✓ embarrassment
✓ anger
✓ inefficiency

Step 1: Recognize that static has entered the listening process.

The first step is to recognize that listening static has entered the process. This means that you must analyze your listening. If you find yourself missing details or zoning in and out of a conversation, lecture, or meeting, admit it.

Step 2: Identify the source

Once you recognize that static is present in the listening process, locate its source. What do you hear, see, or feel that keeps you from listening? Ask, "Why am I having trouble concentrating? Is it the room, the speaker, or the surroundings that distract me?"

Loud noises, people whispering, and other sounds are easy to spot. That's why you hear theater-goers saying, "Sh-h-h-h-h" to people who whisper during a movie.

Other forms of interference are not as identifiable, such as (1) a poor personal or professional relationship with the speaker that biases you against his or her opinions, (2) stresses that overpower your attention while the speaker is talking, (3) feeling ill, (4) worry about a family member, or (5) other reasons.

Step 3: Reduce or eliminate the problem

Is an open window bringing in street sounds? Then close it. Are you angry at the speaker and listening selectively for insults? Try to control your temper and listen to everything that's being said. Are you feeling sick? Ask the speaker if you can discuss the subject at another time. In most, but not all cases, you can control listening static, so it is up to you to make the necessary changes.

If you can't get rid of the distraction, can you avoid looking at it or hearing it? Can you change it in any way? When you are in a situation where you cannot control the static, such as the noise of an airplane landing on a runway, wait for the static to pass and resume your listening.

Step 4: Overcome the distraction

If the listening distraction is something you cannot change, deal with it! Ignore the distraction or develop a strategy of self-talk that helps you refocus your attention on the speaker. You cannot change a speaker's voice or mannerisms, so concentrate on his or her words, focusing your mind on the message instead of on the barriers.

> " Easy listening exists only on the radio. "
>
> — David Barkan

ACTIVITY 3.1

Eliminate the Static

You are the receptionist in a busy hospital emergency room. Activity is going on around you as you try to complete the admitting forms for a new patient. Children cry in the waiting room, an elderly person with a cane wobbles to the water fountain, a visitor stops and asks you for directions, and the phone at the main desk a few feet away keeps ringing. List what you can do to eliminate the static.

Sources of Interference

1. *Crying Children* _____

_____

2. *Elderly person with a cane* _____

_____

3. *Visitor asking directions* _____

_____

4. *Ringing telephone* _____

_____

Ways to Eliminate Interference

Turn the TV in the waiting room to a

children's show _____

_____

_____

_____

_____

_____

_____

_____

External Listening Barriers

Listening barriers can be external or internal. External barriers are often the easiest to identify because they occur from physical roadblocks in the environment. Simply ask yourself "What is it about this room or this situation that makes it hard for me to listen."

For example, if the conference room where staff meetings are held is often hot and stuffy, the chairs are uncomfortable, and telephones and other office noise can be heard through the walls, minimize or eliminate them. The temperature of the room can be adjusted to a comfortable level, new or different chairs can be used in the conference room, telephones can be turned down or turned over to an answering service, and office workers can be requested to be quiet and considerate while the meeting is in progress.

Other physical barriers to listening may include the time of day, weather, hunger pangs, or body fatigue. Since people listen best when they are fresh and alert, schedule an important conference call for the first thing in the morning instead of at 4:30 in the afternoon. If it is snowing outside and the staff is worried about driving home, postpone meetings or conversations to another day and time. For example, a landscape supervisor who schedules a meeting outside then sees storm clouds gathering can change the location of the meeting from outside to inside and minimize distractions.

Physical barriers can also be caused by the speaker. When a waiter tells you the daily specials and speaks too rapidly or uses either a very soft or very loud voice, you encounter a listening barrier the waiter created.

Other physical distractions caused by the speaker may include appearance and mannerisms. Passengers will have trouble listening to the airline pilot who clears his throat, says "uhm", and speaks in a monotone voice over the airplane intercom system. And the sales representative who calls on customers in an unpressed suit, plays with the change in his pocket, glances at his watch every few minutes, or wears tennis shoes with business attire may have trouble getting you to listen. He, too, is causing a listening barrier.

When you are the speaker and you want others to listen to you, how can you avoid becoming the listening barrier? Do the quick self-assessment on the next page to see how you fare.

> "Every person I work with knows something better than me. My job is to listen long enough to find it and use it.
>
> — Jack Nichols

ACTIVITY 3.2

Self-Assessment

For each of the following statements, circle the answer that best describes you when you are the speaker.

1. I wear bright colored clothing, shoes, and accessories to get the listener's attention.   Often   Sometimes   Never

2. I talk loudly when I have something important to say because I get nervous
   and excited.   Often   Sometimes   Never

3. I clear my throat frequently when I am talking.   Often   Sometimes   Never

4. People to whom I talk often comment on my accent.   Often   Sometimes   Never

5. I tend to fidget and move around a lot when I talk.   Often   Sometimes   Never

6. I use many hand gestures when I talk.   Often   Sometimes   Never

7. I do not worry about my appearance because what I have to say is
   more important than how I look.   Often   Sometimes   Never

8. I tend to shuffle my notes while I talk.   Often   Sometimes   Never

9. I try to talk in a monotone voice so I don't give away my personal feelings
   about the topic I'm presenting.   Often   Sometimes   Never

10. People describe me as soft spoken.   Often   Sometimes   Never

11. I talk fast, which means the audience must listen carefully.   Often   Sometimes   Never

12. I skip from subject to subject to keep the audience interested.   Often   Sometimes   Never

13. I believe it is the audience's job to figure out what I'm trying to say.   Often   Sometimes   Never

14. I laugh a lot at my own jokes to get the audience relaxed.   Often   Sometimes   Never

If you answered "often" to more than two of these questions, you may need to work on listening distractions you create. Once you have identified your own problem spots, begin eliminating.

Internal Barriers

Internal listening barriers are roadblocks that people create for themselves. They are things that take place within your own mind and body. You may not be aware of the barriers you have built that prevent effective listening.

Mind barriers can occur when you are stressed or distracted by thoughts of things other than the subject being discussed. Take, for example, Lori, the office manger. When she comes out of her morning meeting, she has a difficult time listening to the secretary who relays phone messages. Lori's thoughts are still on the meeting and the budget cuts her office is about to face. This impairs her ability to listen. When a subject being discussed is overwhelming, too difficult, boring, or too technical, this impedes your listening ability also.

Body barriers such as fatigue, hunger, and sickness can also stand in the way of good listening. For example, Matthew, a human resource specialist, interviews ten people for a receptionist job. By the time he gets to number eleven, he is tired, hungry, and feels a headache coming on. These body barriers prevent Matthew from concentrating on what the job candidate has to say.

Like external barriers, you can control some internal barriers while you may be able only to minimize others.

The key to dealing with these barriers is self-awareness. You can't change what you do not recognize.

> **Only if we restrain ourselves is good conversation possible. Good talk rises upon much discipline.**
>
> — John Erskine

ACTIVITY 3.3

Identifying and Dealing with Distractions

Martha attends a seminar regarding her new health coverage. As the HMO plan is being discussed, Martha thinks the material being covered is unimportant. She is hot, her allergies are bothering her, and she has forgotten to bring a tissue. She can hear a radio outside in the hall and people are talking about their plans for the evening. It is getting late and she is anxious to go home and check on her sick cat. As her mind wanders, Martha notices that the HMO representative has a tear in her hose and keeps trying to cover the hole by pulling at her skirt.

Step No. 1: Recognize the Distraction

What clues tell Martha she is not listening effectively? _____

_____

Step No. 2: Identify the Source

What does Martha see, hear, or feel that keeps her from listening?

See: _____

_____

Hear: _____

_____

Feel: _____

_____

Step No. 3: Eliminate Distractions

Which distractions can Martha eliminate? Which distractions are out of her control? _____

_____

Step No. 4: Make the Change

What can Martha do to reduce or eliminate the distractions? _____

_____

Step No. 5: Overcome the Distraction

Are there any distractions Martha cannot change? What should she do to deal with them, ignore them, or refocus her attention?

_____

_____

Talking is a Barrier to Listening

As odd as it may sound, one of the biggest barriers to listening is talking. That's because talking represents action and power, and society values talking over listening.

In a typical conversation the person talking is in control, so we assume that the talker is powerful and the listener is weak and passive. In fact, effective listening is one way to take charge of a situation. By listening carefully, you can gather information and knowledge that may help you later.

Let's put it this way: If you are talking you couldn't possibly be listening. Tony Alessandra and Phil Hunsaker, in their book *Communicating at Work*, outline four techniques to eliminate talking as a barrier.

Deep breathing. When you feel like talking or interrupting the speaker for any reason, take a deep breath.

Decide to listen. Make a conscious decision to listen to other people. Pay attention and look for interesting, useful things in the conversation.

Paraphrase. Mentally paraphrase what the speaker is saying. Focus your concentration on the speaker and prevent daydreaming.

Eye contact. Maintain eye contact. It's called the hitchhiking theory; where your eyes focus, your ears follow.

Concentrate and Focus on Listening

Take a deep breath.
Make up your mind to listen.
Mentally paraphrase what is being said.
Maintain eye contact with the speaker.

> Opportunities are often missed because we are broadcasting when we should be receiving.
>
> — Author Unknown

GETTING CONNECTED

Use this Website for more information on barriers to listening.

http://www.natsemicom/9706.html

WORKSHOP WRAP-UP

- Become aware of the sources of listening interference.
- Develop strategies for eliminating, controlling or reducing static.
- Listening barriers may be external or internal.
- You can overcome talking as a barrier to listening.

Andre follows his paper broker boss into the office and takes a seat, expecting that what comes next probably will not be pleasant. With a tense face and stern voice, Mr. Foley turns to speak to Andre. "I received a phone call from a customer complaining about the poor treatment she believes she received from you yesterday. Would you like to tell me what happened?"

Andre squirms in his chair. As he explains his side of the story, his body becomes rigid, his lips tighten, and his fists clench. He avoids eye contact with Mr. Foley, raises his voice, takes on an argumentative tone, and increases the speed at which he is talking. "She wanted me to give her a 15 percent discount based on future business she expects to give us. When I told her we can provide only a 5 percent discount until the larger orders come in, she got angry."

Mr. Foley leans back in his chair and says, "That sounds reasonable. So, why is she upset?"

Andre's face reddens, and he makes hand movements for emphasis. "I got mad, too, when she said she would take her business elsewhere, so I told her that would be a good idea. She said she was going to call you, and she walked out."

Mr. Foley, who is now seated, leans back in his chair, peers over the rims of his glasses, and asks, "Why are you still so angry?" after which Andre responds, "I'm not angry."

> " The body is a house of many windows: there we all sit, showing ourselves…"
>
> — Robert Lewis Stevenson

What's Inside

In these pages, you will learn to:

Wordless Communication

Effective listeners focus on more than the speaker's words. They observe non-verbal clues as well. Mr. Foley and Andre's conversation consisted of attitudes and emotions expressed through body language, gestures, and voice.

Understanding the non-verbal elements of communication can be the most important part of listening. Some experts believe that as much as 90 percent of what is communicated between two people in a face-to-face conversation comes from non-verbal cues. Albert Mehrabian states in his article *Communications without Words* that a person's words communicate 7 percent of the story, tone tells 38 percent, and facial expressions, gestures, and posture communicate 55 percent. Has a parent, supervisor, or a teacher ever influenced you through a look?

> ❝ What we learn only through the ears makes less impression upon our mind than what is presented to the trustworthy eye. ❞
>
> — Horace

What Is Non-Verbal Communication?

Non-verbal communication refers to body language and may be more reliable than spoken words because it is an outlet for true, inner feelings. Body language occurs subconsciously when messages are transmitted through eyes, face, hands, arms, legs, and posture and through tone and pace of the voice.

Reading the body language of others can be equated to reading the results of a lie detector test. Unless speakers are actors or have training in non-verbal communication, it is very difficult for them to hide their feelings and attitudes.

As a skilled listener, you should observe facial expressions and body movements to gain insight into what is really being communicated by the speaker. Here are tips for observing body language.

Eyes

Eyes are great communicators. You may roll your eyes to indicate boredom or disbelief, raise your eyebrows to show surprise, or stare for emphasis. People wink to flirt or to let others know when they agree or support them. It is easy to interpret eye gestures because they are used often and are familiar.

Face

The face is an excellent indicator of your true thoughts and emotions. When an attentive store clerk sees the frown and clenched jaws of an unhappy customer, she knows a problem exists, even before the customer opens his mouth. This is a clue to make a neutral or pleasant comment which will disarm the person and reduce tension. On the other hand, the customer who wears a smile from ear to ear communicates a positive mood and attitude and sets the stage for a pleasant conversation.

Hands

Hands are used for emphasis, to give directions, and to serve a variety of other purposes. In combination with facial expressions and eyes, they express surprise, shock, and pleasure. For example, a handshake delivers a courteous introduction, hello, or goodbye. When a co-worker walks down the hall with hands tightly clenched, her stress is apparent.

Arms and Legs

Crossed arms and legs can be negative communication signals. Crossed arms indicate resistance, fear, control, the need for protection, or guardedness. A salesperson who crosses her arms while pitching a product to a customer may not make the sale.

Posture

Your posture when you sit, stand, and walk conveys important clues about how you feel and what you think. Would you rather see a doctor who stands tall and erect with her shoulders back or one who slouches and slumps his shoulders? The doctor with good posture conveys confidence and self-assurance. Slouching sends a message of low self-esteem and low enthusiasm or interest.

Voice

The way you say something frequently means more than what you say. If, for example, the manager of the one-hour photo shop just around the corner from your home uses a gruff and raspy or belligerent voice, customers may prefer to drive a little farther to get their pictures developed by a person who greets them with a friendlier voice.

ACTIVITY 4.1

What is the Message?

Decipher the hidden messages associated with each of the non-verbal actions listed below.

Nonverbal Behavior	Message being communicated
Squinting	
Tapping fingers on desk	
Smiling from ear to ear	
Shaking a fist	
Clapping hands	
Holding hands behind the back	
Scowling	
Swinging a crossed leg	
Pointing an index finger	
Nodding head	
Propping feet on desk	
Raising both eyebrows	
Slouching	
Leaning forward in the chair	

> " What you do speaks so loudly, I cannot hear what you are saying. "
>
> — Unknown

Mixed Messages

When a speaker's words and body language do not match, the resulting mixed message confuses listeners. In such cases, your ability to interpret non-verbal communication becomes doubly important. Most experts trust the non-verbals more than the words.

Nigel stops by his supervisor's office to chat about overtime hours and asks, "Do you have a minute?" The answer, "Sure, I have plenty of time; come on in," sounds inviting. After Nigel enters the office and begins talking, his supervisor glances at his watch, fidgets in his chair, and taps his pen on the desk. Before Nigel finishes his first sentence, his supervisor returns to his stack of papers, making notes and looking up periodically. The mixed message is confusing for Nigel. His best bet is to acknowledge that his supervisor is busy and ask if there is a better time for them to talk. Continuing with the conversation will benefit no one.

As a listener, you need to both listen to the words and observe the non-verbal messages being sent, then react appropriately. Keep in mind that it is easy to choose words to cover or disguise true feelings. It is much harder to cover and disguise non-verbal messages. Observing non-verbal messages will help you figure out what is going on in each listening situation and then make logical, sound decisions from the information obtained.

> There are four ways, and only four ways, in which we have contact with the world. We are evaluated and classified by these four contacts: what we do, how we look, what we say, and how we say it.
>
> — Dale Carnegie

Deciphering the Message

In each situation below, circle the verbal and underline the non-verbal messages. What is the real message in each situation?

1.   "Are you still upset with me for losing that file?" Caroline asks Dan. Dan turns his back toward Caroline then says, "No, don't worry about it."

_____

_____

_____

2.   As a staff meeting is about to begin, Ling, the office manager, walks in looking pale and coughing. During the meeting he slouches in his chair and makes little eye contact. After the meeting, you ask "Are you feeling okay?" Ling shrugs, "I'm feeling fine, don't worry about me."

_____

_____

_____

3.   The small gift shop where you work only accepts cash or credit. Personal checks are not taken because so many bad checks have been received in the past. A customer tries to pay for his purchases with a check and you inform him of the store policy. The customer's body language changes, and he becomes tense and rigid as he begins to dig through his trousers for cash. As you apologize for the inconvenience, the customer snaps, "Don't worry, it's not a problem." He sighs as he retrieves his cash.

_____

_____

_____

4.   "Do I have your permission to take off work one day next week for an appointment to look at a new apartment?" you ask your boss. She looks skeptical, but says, "It's okay this time."

_____

_____

_____

Your Non-Verbal Listening Feedback

Being observant of a speaker's body language is important, but it's equally important to provide non-verbal feedback after you listen. A speaker uses your non-verbal feedback to know whether the message is getting across.

Becoming aware of your own body language is one step to becoming a better listener. Do you look off into space when someone is talking to you? Or glance down at your watch or play with your hair? Do your eyes glaze over? Or do you lean forward to make sure you can hear what is being said? Or sit back with your arms crossed?

ACTIVITY 4.3

The Non-Verbal Messages You Send

For each of the following statements, circle the answer that best describes you. Do you send good non-verbal feedback while you listen?

I listen and do other things at the same time.	Often	Sometimes	Never
I wear a straight face when I listen, showing no emotion or expression.	Often	Sometimes	Never
When I attend lectures or seminars, I slouch in my chair to get comfortable.	Often	Sometimes	Never
People describe me as a stone face. I rarely smile when someone is talking to me.	Often	Sometimes	Never
Making eye contact with the person talking makes me uncomfortable.	Often	Sometimes	Never
I doodle while I listen.	Often	Sometimes	Never
I know I look bored when I listen.	Often	Sometimes	Never
I pretend to be listening, when, in fact, I'm really thinking about something else.	Often	Sometimes	Never
I tap my foot or a pencil when the subject doesn't interest me.	Often	Sometimes	Never

If you answered "often" to more than one of these questions, you may need to work on improving your non-verbal feedback.

Improving Non-Verbal Listening Skill

The following tips from Nan Stutzman Graser, author of *125 Ways to be a Better Listener*, will help you become a better listener.

Face the Speaker

If your back is to the speaker, how does he or she know you are listening? Facing the speaker shows you are interested and paying attention.

Make Eye Contact

Good listeners look into the eyes of the person talking. Making and keeping eye contact connects the speaker and the listener and focuses the conversation.

Use Facial Expressions

Wrinkling your brow and frowning as you listen lets the speaker know you are confused, have questions, or need further explanation. Facial expressions show the speaker how you feel about what you are hearing and seeing.

Display Good Posture

By sitting up straight, you let the speaker know that you are alert and paying attention. Bad posture sends a message of disinterest and boredom.

Take Notes

Write the important points when you listen. Record questions to be asked later, as well as any unclear information or topics of confusion. These notes will not only help you as a listener but will also let the speaker know that you are interested in what is being said.

Avoid Sending Mixed Messages.

Decide what communication you want to send and concentrate on sending it, so that your non-verbal and verbal messages match.

Give Feedback

Good listeners give nonverbal feedback often and consistently during the conversational process, so the speaker can change or adjust the message based on the feedback. If you nod your head in agreement during a meeting, the speaker is encouraged to continue. Looking confused while you flip through the pages of a manual communicates the need for the speaker to clarify a page number or the topic under discussion.

While sending positive messages to the speaker is important, it is equally important to avoid sending negative messages. Negatives distract both the speaker and other listeners.

Positive nonverbal messages

1. Face the speaker.
2. Make eye contact.
3. Sit up straight.
4. Take notes.
5. Use facial expressions.
6. Avoid sending mixed messages.

GETTING CONNECTED

Log on to the Website below and learn more about non-verbal communication.

http:/www.2.pstcc.cc.tn.us/~dking/nvcom.htm

WORKSHOP WRAP-UP

- Body language speaks louder than your words.
- Eyes, face, hands, arms, legs, posture and tone of voice communicate true feelings.
- Skilled listeners listen to the whole message being communicated, both the words and the nonverbal messages.
- Listeners provide feedback to the speaker through their nonverbal messages.

Erick Haden, a self-made millionaire owner of three car washes, gathers his administrative staff at the Malin Road Car Wash for the monthly meeting. Erick plans to discuss the excessive number of repeat car washes that are occurring free of charge because of customer dissatisfaction.

When he first raises the issue, Manley, the wash staff supervisor, becomes defensive and says, "We just have picky customers, Mr. Haden, we can't do anything about that."

Erick, who knows about Manley's defensive attitude, represses his annoyance at the excuse and asks, "If customers are the problem, why do the Tree Side and Park Lane sites show a 45 percent lower re-wash rate?" He adds, "We have to do a good job the first time. We can't afford this return rate."

Manley tries to joke his way out of the situation by saying, "Oh, Mr. Haden, you're a rich man. You can afford it." Then his defensiveness kicks back in, "It's not my fault we're getting these returns. I do my best."

Erick Haden, with blood pressure rising, chokes back his full anger and responds, "Manley, my financial status has nothing to do with whether you and your workers provide high quality service. As a supervisor, the performance of your staff is your responsibility. Next month, when we meet, I expect to see a 25 percent reduction in returns."

Manley, who had no supervisory experience before this job, doesn't hear the last comment because his feelings are hurt, and he's trying to think of something to say to Mr. Haden.

What's Inside

> The principle of listening, someone has said, is to develop a big ear rather than a big mouth.
>
> — Howard G. and Jeanne Hendricks

Travel Through Filters

You bring a set of listening filters into every conversation. As information comes to you from a speaker, it goes through these filters. What you hear may be different from what the speaker intended because your filters change the meaning

Gender, culture, religion, education, personality, physical condition, life experiences, and other factors serve as filters. Just as sunlight becomes distorted as it passes through a filter, words may change from the speaker's meaning when they travel listening filters.

Unique Filters

Each person possesses a set of unique filters that affects his or her listening skill, including such things as memories, values and beliefs, attitudes, assumptions, expectations, strong feelings, and images from the past and for the future. You may not have noticed the filters you and your associates carry around.

Alex, a new employee at a grocery store, serves as an example of a person whose listening filters interfere with conversation. Alex's supervisor frowns on casual conversation and socializing during the restocking of shelves. He believes that work goes more slowly when workers talk as they restock. Alex believes he works harder and gets more done when he jokes around while he stocks, a behavior that his supervisor interprets as goofing off. Because they have different attitudes and

expectations, Alex and his supervisor are disappointed and frustrated with each other's work habits.

Listening filters can be explained best by comparing them to filters that water goes through to be purified. Some water is saved, other water is recycled for additional filtering, and some with impurities doesn't make it through the filter at all. As a listener, you accept some comments as presented, but you run others through mental filters where the message is adjusted by your experiences and attitudes.

A brief listing and discussion of listening filters will help you understand the role they play in communication.

Memories

Good and bad memories of past experiences cloud your thinking. For example, if your child's day care director reminds you of your third grade teacher, a person you remember as mean and bossy, your listening will be colored by the memories.

Values

All information you receive filters through your personal value system, and you interpret what you hear based on these values. If your parents taught that children should be seen and not heard, customers with loud and boisterous children may not receive your full attention because you focus on the behavior of their children.

Interests

Subjects that interest you get your ear. If you are not interested, you may flip through the information quickly and maintain only the part that is appealing. For example, if you are not interested in sports, you may change television channels during the evening news when the sportscaster comes on.

Strong Feelings

Strong feelings on a subject directly relate to a listener's objectivity. When you become involved in a subject that you are passionate about, your objectivity may disappear. Religion and politics are two hot topics that cause listeners trouble.

Beliefs

A lifetime of beliefs, some taken from family and cultural background, influence what a listener hears. A worker who comes from a culture that values family, including extended family, may not understand when you tell her that she will not be allowed to take several weeks off to be with her dying grandmother.

Expectations

When the performance expectations of the speaker and the listener don't match, the listener tends to hear the words that satisfy his or her need. If you drop your lawn mower off for repair at the local hardware store and the clerk tells you it will be ready by Saturday, you may ask for a loaner because you expect the repairs to take longer.

Past and Future Images

Good and bad past experiences play a part in what is heard. If two cable installers have been to your home and neither has been able to provide clear reception, you may listen skeptically when a third installer explains the problem.

Typical Listening Filters

Memories	Beliefs
Values	Expectations
Interests	Attitudes
Strong Feelings	Assumptions
Past Experiences	Interests
Physical Environment	Prejudices
Past & Future Images	

Listening: The Forgotten Skill
Madelyn Burley-Allen

Focus on Filters

Case Study No. 1 provides an example of how filters influence one person's listening. After studying this example, read Case Study No. 2 and write the filters that affect the listener.

Case Study No. 1

Enrique hopes to own his own landscaping business some day; but for now, he works at Van's Nursery and goes to school part-time. Just as he's leaving work and heading for his daily basketball game, his supervisor stops him to discuss overtime hours this weekend. He knows Enrique lives with his mother and would like to get his own place. The following filters affect Enrique's listening ability:

Case No. 2

Anita's car is making a funny noise again, bringing back memories of the bad experience she had the last time her car was in the shop. She explains to the mechanic that she can't miss another day of work because of car problems, and she inquires about the cost of the repairs. Her savings account is low and her credit card is full. The mechanic says, "We'll do our best to be fast so you can get your car back and keep the expenses down."

Write in the ovals the filters that affect Anita's listening skills as she talks with the mechanic.

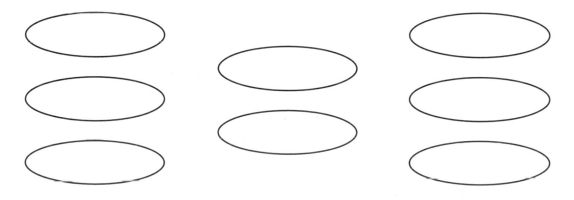

Dealing with Listening Filters

To improve your listening skills, first learn as much as you can about your listening filters. Then study the filters of the people you communicate with at home and work. Listen without judgment to what they say and provide feedback that fits what you know about them. Becoming aware of the listening filters of others will enable you to make assumptions about how to give and receive information when you find yourself in a listening situation.

> " The older I get the more I listen to people who don't talk much. "
>
> — Germaina G. Glien

ACTIVITY 5.2

Identify Your Listening Filters

One way to improve your listening skills is to identify and understand your own unique listening filters that have developed over a lifetime. Identify ten of your listening filters:

Listening Filters

1. *Female* _____
2. *Southern born* _____
3. _____
4. _____
5. _____
6. _____
7. _____
8. _____
9. _____
10. _____

Quick Skills

GETTING CONNECTED

Log on to the Internet and visit the USA Weekend Website to locate an article about a person involved in a listening situation.

http://www.usaweekend.com/

How would you adjust your communications with this person based on what you know about their listening filters?

WORKSHOP WRAP-UP

- People listen through filters.
- What individuals hear is based on a lifetime of experiences and attitudes.
- Identifying your unique listening filters is the first step to improving listening skills.
- Understanding the filters of those around you improves listening skills.

BECOME A BETTER LISTENER

Lena locates a piece of paper and begins to take lengthy notes about the new 401K plan the speaker is discussing. Although Lena is tired, her headache has returned, and she still has to get one more report filed before she can call it a day, she concentrates on what Maria is saying. She repeats Maria's words to herself as she writes the key points. When she finds her mind drifting, she conscientiously brings herself back to the topic and focuses on the key words she writes in her notes.

Instead of interrupting Maria with questions, Lena jots them down as they occur to her. When the right opportunity comes, she will ask her questions. She doesn't want to get the speaker or the other listeners off track. So far, the topic has been well organized and thoughtfully presented. Lena plans to participate fully in the 401K so she can be financially secure at retirement, and distracting the speaker would not be to her advantage.

Lena wants to display the habits of a good listener. Even though she experiences distractions that could keep her from listening, she continues to focus her attention on the speaker. She has learned from past experience that having good listeners helps a speaker convey information effectively.

What's Inside

In these pages, you will learn to:

> " Let them see you listening. "
>
> — Rick Phillips
> Sales Doctor's Magazine

Being a Good Listener Is Important

No matter what type of work you do, you will have an edge over co-workers if you are a good listener. Employees who listen are more productive and contribute better ideas than poor listeners. They progress faster in their careers than their co-workers who lack this skill.

Good listeners recognize valuable information and act on it to make informed decisions. Since information represents power, good listeners are powerful people.

When you listen effectively, you create an environment of cooperation. Others feel respected and comfortable in your presence. They open up and provide valuable insights, opinions, and points of view. Friends and co-workers develop a positive attitude toward you and like to be in your presence. Although listening takes time, it saves time in the long run by reducing mistakes, repetition, and misunderstandings.

ACTIVITY 6.1

Listening Check

Ask a partner to read one of the entries below to you. On the lines, summarize what you heard; then answer the questions after each summary.

Situation 1

A customer comes in one day complaining about a loud and recurring noise in her car. She says two other shops in the area have failed to fix the problem. She describes the different repairs she has done previously, and mentions the amount of money and time she has spent. The noise persists, and in fact, is getting worse. She worries about the car and is frustrated that the problem cannot be solved.

Summary: _____

_____

_____

Read the summary to your partner. Does your partner believe you captured all the points? _____ Yes _____ No

Did any distractions interfere with listening? _daydreaming, noises from outside_____

_____

How can you improve your listening? _____

_____

_____

Entry 2:

Today's buyers are smarter, tougher, and more demanding. They are increasingly impatient with poor products and services, and they don't think twice about taking their business elsewhere when they are dissatisfied. Consequently, to make a profit, companies and the people who work for these companies must figure out what their customers want and need. Then they have to find a way to meet those needs with excellent products and superior service.

Summary: _____

_____

_____

Read the summary to your partner. Does your partner believe you captured all the points? _____ Yes_____No

How can you improve your listening? _____

_____

_____

_____

_____

Develop a Positive Listening Attitude

Your attitude can have an effect on your ability to listen. If you think negatively, you will listen negatively; and if you think positively, you will listen positively. When you find a negative attitude influencing your listening, follow a few easy steps to turn things around.

Keep your attitude in check

Before you start to listen, ask yourself how you feel about the speaker and the subject. If preconceived notions come to mind, admit them; and place them in a mental file drawer so they will not influence your listening. Ask yourself, "What is my attitude? Do I need to change it?"

Become aware of your self-talk

We all talk mentally to ourselves. These messages can be powerful, having a tremendous impact on your attitude. If you catch yourself thinking negatively, such as "This is really boring. I can't wait to get out of here," turn this self-talk into a positive message. Say to yourself, "I should pay attention because I might learn something new."

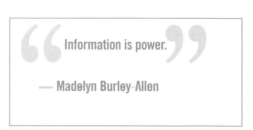

Keep an open mind

By freeing your mind of judgments regarding the speaker and the topic being discussed, you will have a more open, positive attitude. Avoid jumping to conclusions and making judgments until you've listened to the entire message.

Look for the positive in the message

As you listen, search through the message to find information that will impact you positively. For example, your supervisor talks about the additional hours everyone will work to meet the upcoming deadline, think about the advantages of earning extra money.

Look for new ideas

The non-judgmental attitudes of good listeners allow them to respond to new ideas, practices, and policies. When you listen with a positive attitude, new ideas and innovative ways of doing things will jump out.

> " Information is power. "
> — Madelyn Burley-Allen

Attitudes and listening

In each of the following situations, a negative attitude exists. Suggest ways to turn the negative attitude into a positive one.

1. During a training session for new employees, you are shown a safety film and asked to listen to the safety guidelines. You think, "This is boring. Wake me up when it's over."

_____

_____

_____

2. Your store manager calls you over to talk about next week's schedule. You worry about your plans to attend a concert with your friends next week. You think, "Oh no, if he thinks I'm going to work extra hours next Thursday night, he's wrong!"

_____

_____

_____

3. You notice the luncheon speaker is wearing a light blue suit that looks like it came straight out of his father's decades old closet. You slump in your chair and think to yourself, "How can this guy have anything to say that I want to hear? Another wasted $25."

_____

_____

_____

4. The staff meeting has already gone 30 minutes over the scheduled time and there's no end in sight. Your mind is wandering and you say to yourself, "I have to get out of here. I have a million things waiting for me back at my desk."

_____

_____

_____

5. Your supervisor gives you a new assignment. You think, "I wish he would ask someone else. I have enough to do."

_____

_____

_____

Good Listeners Ask Questions

As a listener, you have a responsibility to try to understand what is being said. Asking the speaker to repeat information, give examples, or provide further explanation are all good questioning techniques. No question is silly if it clarifies the message.

Asking questions means you are a smart listener. However, learning how to ask the right questions at the right time will improve your listening skills.

Timing is everything

A question pops into your head and exits right from your mouth, interrupting the speaker and causing him to lose his train of thought. You distracted not only the speaker but everyone else who is trying to listen. This is rude and also works against your goal of understanding the topic, as the speaker has to pause to collect his thoughts after answering your question. Hold your questions until the appropriate time.

Write your questions

When your mind races with questions and they begin to run together in your head, grab your note pad and begin writing. This way, you don't have to worry about forgetting any of your questions, and you can wait until the speaker has finished before asking them.

Ask specific questions

Vague, general questions may not produce the answers that will help you clarify or understand the speaker's message. Ask clear, specific questions that pinpoint your lack of understanding, so the speaker can refocus the message. "What does that mean?" should be replaced with "Does 'soon' mean next week or next month?"

Keep questions on the topic

Smart listeners keep their questions to the current topic being discussed and ask unrelated questions at a different time. When Mary, who is tired of hearing about safety on the job, asks a question about the vacation schedule, she distracts her supervisor and her co-workers who are trying to listen.

Ask for definitions

Smart listeners let the speaker know when they do not understand words, phrases, or unfamiliar terms. If the speaker uses technical terms and acronyms unfamiliar to you, do not go along with the conversation and pretend you understand everything being said.

Simply say, "What does protocol mean?" or "I don't understand the term EIS. Could you please explain?" This shows that you are listening and that you are interested.

Ask speakers to repeat

As hard as you try to concentrate, there are times when you will miss the message. Outside distractions, daydreaming, and poor acoustics are reasons to ask speakers to repeat what they say. It is okay to acknowledge that you missed something. Make the comment, "Could you please repeat what you just said. I missed that."

Ask for explanations

Restating what you think the speaker said is a valuable technique for ensuring that you understand the message. When Carmen is confused about the new return policy the store plans to initiate, she says to the store manager "I'm confused about that new policy. Can you explain it again?"

By asking for further explanation, you can avoid confusion, misunderstandings, hurt feelings, and unhappy customers. The box below offers more hints for good questioning:

> The best way to persuade people is with your ears by listening to them.
>
> —— Dean Rusk

Ask Questions

- at the right time
- in a specific manner
- to get information on the topic
- to learn definitions
- to get information repeated
- to get explanations

Asking Questions

Read each message to yourself. As you listen to the message, record questions that will clarify what is being said.

1. Get this copied as soon as possible.

   How many copies do you need?

   When do you need it?

   _____

2. The marketing team will meet at 9 a.m. and will work most of the day together.

   _____

   _____

   _____

3. I expect everyone to be here bright and early tomorrow. Wear comfortable clothing because we have a lot of work to do.

   _____

   _____

   _____

4. Deliver this package to Mr. Smith. Take the main hallway, then take the central elevator. His office is the last one at the end of the west wing.

   _____

   _____

   _____

5. I would like you to redo this report. Read each of the paragraphs, delete extraneous information, leave the acceptable paragraphs, and insert the appropriate graphs within the text.

   _____

   _____

   _____

Practice Listening

Becoming an effective listener is much like getting your body into shape. It starts with identifying the areas that need work, developing a goal, then prescribing how to improve those areas to reach your goal. The best way to put your plan into action is to practice. Practice your listening skills at home, with friends, and at work.

Practice listening

Do
Listen with understanding.
Look the speaker in the eye.
Face the speaker with a relaxed posture.
Acknowledge that you are listening through your body language.
Nod your head.
Display facial expressions that match the message.
Ask questions to clarify what the speaker is saying.

Do not
Be judgmental or critical as you listen.
Interrupt.
Fidget or cause distractions to the speaker or other listeners.
Ask questions that distract the speaker.

> A good listener tries to understand what the other person is saying. In the end, he may disagree sharply; but because he disagrees, he wants to know exactly what he is disagreeing with.
>
> — Roger G. Imhoff

For more information on good listening, log on to the Internet and visit the Web site "Attributes of Good Listening," which can be found at:

http://www.ssu.missouri.edu/faculty/rcampbell/Leadership/chapter6.htm

Here you will find thirteen attributes of good listening. Exploring each attribute will allow you to further improve your listening skills.

WORKSHOP WRAP-UP

- Effective listeners perform better.
- Your attitude affects your ability to listen.
- You can change negative listening by focusing on the positive in a conversation.
- Good listeners ask questions to gain a better understanding of the speaker.
- The best way to become a good listener is to practice listening.

GETTING OTHERS TO LISTEN

On Monday morning, Lori feels frustrated and overwhelmed about her long hours and low pay, so she decides to talk to the day care director. Trying to make him understand how badly she needs money, she describes her expenses, including her apartment rent and car payment. The director pretends to pay attention, but Lori can tell that his mind is elsewhere.

Determined to get things settled, Lori schedules another meeting for Tuesday. This time she reminds him of how long she has worked at the center and implies that he is being unfair if he does not increase her pay. Growing braver, at one point she asks, "Are you listening to me?"

She's shocked when he responds, "Lori, you're whining, and that makes it hard to listen. All of our employees would like more money. I can't justify additional salaries based on your personal needs. Why don't you prepare a list of the positive effects on the day care center if we increase your salary?"

Lori is first angry, then embarrassed. Later, as she remembers the conversation, she realizes that she probably came across as self-interested. She actually loves the children, and they ask for her each morning when they are dropped off. The parents like her, too, and frequently compliment her skill in handling the day-to-day crises. She wants to stay at the center, but she will need to look for another job unless she gets a salary increase soon. She decides to take the director's advice and make a list of the reasons why he should increase her salary. Maybe, then, she will get his attention.

What's Inside

In these pages, you will learn to:

Listen to Yourself

The previous workshops have focused on you as a listener. Another powerful element of listening is getting others to listen to you when you speak. Two steps will help you.

Step 1. Show sincerity

The first step to gaining a listener's attention is to be a good listener yourself. When you listen attentively to friends or co-workers, they sense your sincerity. When your turn comes to speak, they will listen—if not out of desire, then out of respect.

Step 2. Identify your barriers

The second step is to identify any of your behaviors that make you a bad speaker. For example, Marlene who is locating directions so she can deliver an order to a new customer is interrupted when Evan blurts out a shortcut. Marlene keeps her eyes on the map and continues to chart her route. She chooses not to listen to Evan's directions because he annoyed her with unsolicited assistance.

As a speaker, choose when to speak. When you give unwanted advice, others may choose to ignore you. Unless they imply they want help or make a direct request for assistance, refrain from offering suggestions. At the least, ask, "May I offer a suggestion?" Your listener then has a choice.

Knowing what listeners reject is as important as knowing what encourages them. Think back to times when someone spoke to you and you resisted their comments. Do you duplicate any of this person's speaking behaviors?

Getting a listener's attention

Before people can listen, you must have their attention. You can use words, behavior, voice, attitude, questions, and feedback to gain attention.

Choice of words

The words you use contribute to the listener's desire to hear your message. As with all good communicators, most of your words should be positive. When you need to discuss a negative, adjust the words so the message is stated in a positive way. Instead of saying, "You put that report together carefully," say, "This report is a good beginning; now I would like you to organize and finish it."

By simply choosing your words carefully, you will gain better listeners. Speakers who refer to problems or mistakes as "challenges" not only speak in more positive terms, but they avoid flag words that cause listening resistance. Using a question to address a negative also helps. For example, "Did you run out of time to finish this report?"

Negative flag words that encourage listening problems and their positive replacement words or phrases are shown in the chart below.

Negative Flag Words	Positive Replacement
Problem	Challenge
Mistake	Overlooked a point
Poor	A few changes needed
Negligent	Pay attention to detail
Unacceptable	Redo

Non-Verbal Behavior

You learned in Workshop 4 how to overcome the distractions of a speaker's non-verbal behaviors. Analyze the non-verbal behaviors you exhibit when you speak and apply the guidelines in Workshop 4 to yourself. Consider how Thomas, described below, created a listening problem.

With a scowl, red face, and rapidly rising voice, Thomas shakes his finger at Jake and describes the plumbing problems that will no go away. Although Jake has been a plumber for years and is used to dealing with upset customers, Thomas' non-verbal behavior implies that he may be a physically dangerous customer if he does not approve of Jake's work. Jake cannot listen about the plumbing because he is anxious about his safety.

Your Tone of Voice

Your tone of voice communicates more than your words. Whether you talk to associates or customers, adjust your tone to the situation.

When you greet a listener upon arrival in your office, use a warm pleasant voice; however, if your goal is to make a strong point, use a forceful, confident tone. Avoid hard, sharp, and sarcastic tones.

Your Attitude

Attitudes are contagious. Is yours worth catching?

By showing a positive attitude, you encourage people to trust you. They want to hear what you have to say and are likely to listen. As you speak, be sincere. Avoid unnecessary criticism, empty compliments and judgmental statements. Say what you mean and mean what you say.

Carolyn, an interior decorator and manager of the business, is known as an excellent manager.

She displays a positive attitude about her work, and the people around her know that she is sincere. When she speaks, she means what she says.

> **Your attitude speaks so loudly, I can't hear what you are saying.**
>
> — Anonymous

Questions

When you speak, ask your listener a question occasionally to ensure that the person understands what you are saying and to obtain ideas and draw out any reservations the person may have about what you are saying. Most people prefer to participate in conversations; by asking a question, you give the listener an opportunity to offer an opinion or make a statement. When listeners know you will engage them in the dialogue, they are more motivated to pay attention and stay involved as a listener.

Philippe, a warehouse manager, provides a good example. He knows the monthly warehouse staff meetings are dull and boring and that the workers aren't paying attention to what he says. This month he plans to conduct the meeting differently. As he covers each item on the agenda, he asks the warehouse workers a few questions and solicits their ideas and thoughts. This technique not only gets the workers' attention, but they also elicit suggestions Phillipe uses to improve productivity.

Feedback

When you are the speaker, getting questions from your listeners provides valuable feedback. How you use the feedback determines whether your listener continues to participate in the conversation. If you ignore the feedback and continue to talk about your views instead of altering the message to address the listener's concerns, you will lose the individual's trust. Roxanne provides a good example.

Roxanne reviews the new ordering system for parts with a group of supervisors, then asks the group if they have any ideas on how to train the other employees on the new system. When Jim makes a suggestion, Roxanne thanks him for his information and continues to outline her own plan. By doing this, she communicates to Jim and the group that, while she asks for ideas, she does not actually want them. She already has her mind made up. Jim feels foolish that he spoke up and is unlikely to volunteer when Roxanne asks a question in the future.

People listen to your

- ✓ Words
- ✓ Behavior
- ✓ Voice
- ✓ Attitude
- ✓ Questions
- ✓ And the way you handle the answers to their questions

Why Didn't He Listen?

Analyze Brandon's behavior in the situation below and describe why his supervisor was not motivated to listen. Reword Brandon's remarks in a way that will encourage his supervisor to listen.

Brandon walks into this supervisor's office with his arms crossed over his chest and says impatiently, "We've got a problem. I can't service the Wadsworth account without more help. This job is too big for one person to do alone, and I have brought it up to you twice before." Mohammed, the supervisor, continues working on his laptop computer and responds,"Uh huh."

Why didn't Mohammed listen to what Brandon had to say?

Brandon starts the conversation with negative words _____

_____

_____

Reword Brandon's remarks so Mohammed will listen.

_____

_____

_____

_____

_____

> " Talk to a man about himself and he will listen for hours. "
>
> — Benjamin Disraeli

Your Turn to Talk

When it's your turn to talk, be prepared to use your listener's time advantageously. Four talking tips for getting others to listen are discussed below:

- ◆ Be ready to talk
- ◆ Know your listener
- ◆ Make sure the listener understands
- ◆ Encourage feedback

> " It is difficult for anyone to speak when you listen only to yourself. "
>
> — Lorna Bounty

Be ready to talk

Know what message you are trying to convey and be clear in your delivery. Listeners become bored, impatient, and disinterested when a speaker rambles.

Before the monthly staff meeting, Julie makes an outline of the things she needs to discuss with employees, including such items as the distribution of insurance cards, a newly designed prescription form, and changes in the dental coverage. By making a quick outline, she organizes how she is going to cover the information. She uses the employees' time efficiently and sends a clear message.

Know your listener

The more you know about your audience or listeners the better you will be at gaining their attention. The key is to focus on their needs and interests as you talk.

When Sabina approaches her supervisor about reducing her hours so she can return to school part-time, she emphasizes how finishing her degree will make her a better employee and help the company in the long run. She knows her request will be met more positively if she refrains from focusing on the personal benefits.

Make sure the listener understands

A good speaker starts by presenting information simply and adds ideas or new information in small doses.

Mac uses technical terms and computer jargon as he gives Regina detailed instructions about developing formulas for spreadsheet. After a while, she begins to fidget and doodle on her notepad. Mac recognizes she is no longer listening.

Mac's language is not appropriate for his audience. Regina needs basic information on how to set up a spreadsheet, but what Mac provides is too technical and goes over her head. She becomes confused and loses interest. Mac should adjust his terminology to speak in terms that Regina can understand.

Encourage feedback

Encourage listeners to co-own the conversation by asking for their feedback. Respond to the feedback that is given, then ask for more feedback.

Mary, who spends most of her time providing customers with telephone technical support, often asks questions relating to the problem. Without feedback and interaction from her customers, Mary does not know whether they are following her explanations and solutions.

What Will You Say?

Two situations are described below. Think about how you would handle each and provide the information requested.

Situation 1

You have been promoted to the assistant manager of an apartment complex. Your first task is to interview a prospective maintenance employee. You have never conducted an interview before, but you do not want the applicant to know.

Prepare an outline of the points you will cover.

_____

_____

_____

_____

_____

Situation 2

As the owner of a dry cleaning business, you need to talk to one of your employees about his tardiness to work. Create an outline of the points you will cover.

_____

_____

_____

_____

_____

> " The art of conversation consists as much in listening politely as in talking agreeably. "
>
> — Atwell

Stick to the Facts

When you talk, stick to the facts. Avoid presenting your opinion or the opinion of others as fact, and refuse to participate in gossip or rumor; otherwise, you will lose credibility. Avoid generalizations. Ask questions like How? When? Where? and Why? This will keep your thoughts and ideas on track so that the listener can understand.

Nancy, an office manager is uncomfortable with the results of a job performance appraisal she conducts with Ramon. He answers each question with long, drawn-out statements that are very vague and general, which confuses her. She thinks to herself "What is more distracting, what he has to say or the way he mumbles his way through the conversation?"

Ramon makes several critical mistakes during this interview. When he speaks, he should be clear and concise. By talking too much, he loses Nancy's attention. Ramon also became a distraction to himself.

Mean What You Say

Another way to motivate others to listen to you is to mean what you say and follow through with what you say you will do. Never make promises, threats, or statements that you have no intention of carrying out.

Frustrated at the slow pace of the construction crew, Hardy threatens to cut out any overtime pay in the future. He knows he cannot stand by his threat because there will be times when overtime will be required to get jobs finished on time. His crew also knows his threat is empty, so they ignore his comments.

Talking Do's and Don't's

Use the chart below to help yourself become an effective speaker so your listeners will listen.

Ask Questions

Talking Do's	Talking Don'ts
Deal with facts.	Don't state opinions as facts.
Stick to the facts.	Don't participate in gossip or rumor.

Describe the situation—
  "He talks loudly."
	Don't use judgmental descriptions—
	  "He is a loudmouth."

Be clear and concise.	Don't drag things out.
Be specific.	Don't generalize.
Say what you mean.	Don't use idle threats or make false promises.
Eliminate or control distractions.	Don't be the cause or source of distractions.

ACTIVITY 7.3

Self-Assessment

Complete the self-assessment below to determine whether you are an effective speaker who encourages listeners to hear what you say.

1. When I talk, I have a clear picture of what I am going to say.	Never	Sometimes	Always
2. I follow through on things I say I am going to do.	Never	Sometimes	Always
3. I am aware of my own nonverbal behavior while I am talking.	Never	Sometimes	Always
4. I avoid conversations that involve gossip.	Never	Sometimes	Always
5. As I speak, I ask questions to involve the listeners.	Never	Sometimes	Always
6. I try to talk to people on their level without talking over their heads or talking down to them.	Never	Sometimes	Always
7. I don't use negative words or phrases when I talk.	Never	Sometimes	Always
8. I try to talk about things that are important to the listener.	Never	Sometimes	Always
9. I adapt or adjust what I am saying based on the feedback I receive from the people I am talking to.	Never	Sometimes	Always
10. I convey a positive attitude when I speak.	Never	Sometimes	Always
11. When I talk, I keep my conversations clear and concise.	Never	Sometimes	Always
12. I use a professional tone of voice when I am at work.	Never	Sometimes	Always

If you answered "always" to all twelve statements, then you probably gain your listener's attention. If you answered "sometimes" or "never" to any of the statements, you need to work on your speaking habits in order to get others to listen to you.

> " The time to stop talking is when the other person nods affirmatively but says nothing. "
>
> — Unknown

Investigate this Website for suggestions on making an effective presentation by getting Website people to listen to you.

http://www.infoworld.com/cgi-bin,displayStat.pl?careers/980/26present.htm

WORKSHOP WRAP-UP

- When you listen to others, they are more likely to listen to you.
- Your choice of words, nonverbal behavior, tone of voice, attitude, and questions determine the level of attention listeners give you.
- People listen to speakers who are prepared. Being prepared to speak means knowing what you are going to say and knowing your audience.
- Speak in facts. Avoiding gossip, criticisms, and judgmental statements. You can increase your ability to get others to listen to you by being clear, concise, and specific.

Deena answers the phone and hears an angry customer saying, "Why didn't you return my call? I have an emergency, and I've been waiting for over an hour." Once Deena has calmed the customer and taken care of the crisis, she walks over to Juan's desk and asks, "Juan, did you take any messages for me while I was at lunch?"

Juan gasps and says "I'm sorry, I forgot. I was busy working on a report when the call came in so I didn't write it down. I can probably remember most of what the person said. He will call back if the message was important."

"That was an important customer calling and he had a critical situation," Deena replies, trying to hold her annoyance in check at Juan's lack of responsibility for her telephone message. We may lose his business if he perceives we're not giving him good service."

Juan knows he made a mistake by not writing the message and leaving it on Deena's desk. While he can recall part of what the man said, he knows he cannot remember the full conversation. Since the person was not his client, he did not pay much attention.

In the past, Juan has failed to record messages for other staff members. One time the supervisor sent him to a day-long seminar of good telephone techniques. He's aware that poor telephone follow through is creating problems in his job.

What's Inside

In these pages, you will learn to:

Importance of the Telephone

The telephone is an old, familiar friend. We take its use for granted because we have always known the telephone.

Telephones are the lifeline of our personal and professional lives. Every day you see people talking on the phone as they travel in their cars or in airplanes, as they shop for groceries, and walk down the street. Cellular technology has made the telephone a tool we are never without.

In today's technology-based workplace, getting accurate information quickly is vital to any company's success. Although there are many ways to get and retrieve information, the telephone remains at the top of the list, with employees using the telephone for one task or another in almost every job.

Whether you take incoming orders at a pizza parlor, work the help desk for a computer software company, or conduct customer sales calls, the telephone is an important tool in your work and in your relationship with others.

Use the telephone effectively, and you will save time, create good will, and maintain contact with important associates and customers.

During a business call, the impression you give over the telephone becomes the impression the caller receives of the company. Because the telephone is such an important tool, companies spend hundreds of thousands of dollars a year training their staff to use it correctly.

When you meet and talk to people face to face, they form an impression of you from your appearance, behavior, body language, and voice. However, when the conversation is by telephone, callers know you only through your voice. Because they are unable to see you, the non-verbal aspect of the communication process is missing. From previous workshops, you know how important non-verbal feedback is to any conversation, so you must be extremely conscious of telephone techniques that improve your communication.

To be an effective telephone conversationalist, you should put a smile in your voice. You can make your voice smile by applying a few basic principles of listening. First, complete the activity below to learn more about your telephone habits.

> " I like to listen. I have learned a great deal from listening carefully. Most people never listen. "
>
> — Ernest Hemingway

First Impressions

Read each statement below and check the category which best describes your telephone habits.

1.	I jot down notes and take written messages from callers.	Often	Sometimes	Never
2.	I treat callers as I would like to be treated during a telephone conversation.	Often	Sometimes	Never
3.	I keep a pad of paper and a pencil next to the phone.	Often	Sometimes	Never
4.	I never chew gum, eat, or drink while I am on the phone.	Often	Sometimes	Never
5.	I use a normal rate of speech, talking slowly enough that the caller can understand what I am saying.	Often	Sometimes	Never
6.	I ask questions to clarify the information being given.	Often	Sometimes	Never
7.	I often repeat and rephrase what the caller is saying during the conversation.	Often	Sometimes	Never
8.	I use a polite, business-like tone of voice when I am on the telephone.	Often	Sometimes	Never
9.	I use the caller's name in the conversation to show interest and concern.	Often	Sometimes	Never
10.	I regularly say "please" and "thank you" during telephone conversations.	Often	Sometimes	Never

If you selected "seldom" or "never" for any of the statements, then you should improve your telephone skills.

> " This 'telephone' has too many shortcomings to be seriously considered as a means of communication. The device is inherently of no value to us. "
>
> — Western Union

How to Listen to a Caller

A telephone conversation deserves the same attention you would give the speaker if you were talking to them face to face. Whether the caller is a personal or professional acquaintance, he or she deserves your full attention.

As you take and make phone calls during the day, do you pay attention to what's being said? Do you ask questions and take notes during the conversation? Or do you type a report, make a list of things you need to accomplish, and clean up your desk while the conversation is taking place?

Five effective telephone listening techniques are shown in the box below and discussed in the following paragraphs. Many are similar to the listening techniques used in face-to-face situations; however, their intensity should be increased during telephone conversations where non-verbal feedback is missing.

Effective Telephone Listening Techniques

✓ Concentrate.
✓ Listen for main ideas.
✓ Ask questions for clarification.
✓ Rephrase and repeat what you hear.
✓ Write it down.

Concentrate

The first step to improving your telephone listening skill is to concentrate on the words being spoken. This means giving your full attention to the speaker and discontinuing other activities.

Listen for main ideas

Although it is important to try to listen to most of the caller's words, good telephone listeners focus on the main ideas. Listen for important information and avoid being overwhelmed by unnecessary details and side comments.

Ask questions

You hear what the caller is saying, but do you understand what is meant? If not, ask open-ended questions that cannot be answered "yes" or "no." This alerts the caller to explain further. Start with the basic questions: Who? What? Where? When? Why? or How?

Repeat what you hear

Clarify what you hear by repeating the information. For example, "Did you say the best time for the meeting is Friday, January 17, at 3 o'clock?" Repeating word for word is not necessary. Instead, try rephrasing, putting the message in your own words, and relaying it back to the speaker. This not only helps you understand what is being said, but provides the speaker with feedback.

Write it down

Relying strictly on memory to convey messages is not a good idea. To avoid confusion, inaccurate, or missed messages, be prepared to take notes about what is said.

Listening for the Main Idea

Pick out the important information in each of the messages below. Then, in your own words, rephrase the message in the space provided.

1. A patient calls a doctor's office and complains about not feeling well. She says, "I think I have the flu. I have a fever of 102 and a tight cough. I stood out in the rain yesterday, but not for long. Before I went to bed I took some aspirin, and it made me feel better."

_____

_____

_____

2. Chris explains to his car mechanic, "My car makes a banging noise when I apply the brakes. It also vibrates and squeaks when I go over 55 mph. I tried to fix the brakes myself; and when I got underneath, I saw a bunch of things that didn't look right."

_____

_____

_____

3. During a meeting between a homeowner and a landscape designer, the homeowner explains, "I have a budget of $500. I love to work in the yard but have very little time to spend maintaining it. I want it to look great with lots of exotic plants, bushes and trees. You can use your judgment about which ones to plant. I need everything finished for a July 4 party."

_____

_____

_____

4. A nurse discusses a prescription with a patient and says, "Be sure to take this medicine with food. Without food, you may get an upset stomach. Drink plenty of water. When you have a chance, come back in and have your annual check up. It has been a year since you had a thorough examination. I'll call you about the exam if you forget."

_____

_____

_____

Strategies for Remembering Messages

Three strategies will help you remember telephone messages. Practice using these each time you engage in a telephone conversation, and they will become a habit.

Repeat Words or Ideas to Yourself

Self-talk is an important tool in helping you remember telephone conversations. By repeating words, phrases, sentences, or whole ideas to yourself, you hear the information more than once and, therefore, will be more likely to remember it.

Use the Information in Your Response

To remember a person's name and the information conveyed, repeat the individual's name and some of the information in your response. Say, "I'm sorry your having trouble with this account, Mr. Yu. Let me repeat your account number—that's X2C48328. Correct?"

Create a mental picture

As you listen, create a mental picture or image of what is being discussed. For example, if a customer is calling about a open house you are arranging for his new building, picture the layout he describes. In your mind, place the furniture at the locations he designates.

Creating a mental picture is a powerful memory tool that can remind you of names, numbers, dates, and times. This is similar to self-talk. You will be getting the same information more than once and will be more likely to remember it.

> If the person you are talking to doesn't appear to be listening, be patient. It may simply be that he has a small piece of fluff in his ear.
>
> — *Pooh's Little Instruction Book*

ACTIVITY 8.3

Listening on the job

Read each of the job descriptions below, then complete the statement, answer the question, or give the listener some advice.

1.   Margaret works as a travel agent and handles many large corporate accounts. Some days, she makes over 100 travel plans. What listening advice would you give her?

_____

_____

_____

2.   Thomas is a customer service representative for a mail order catalog. His main responsibility is to take customer catalog orders over the phone. He takes catalog numbers, item numbers, quantity, color, size, credit card information, and mailing instructions with each order. Describe why Thomas' listening skills on the job are important.

_____

_____

_____

3.   A 911 operator answers a caller in distress. What advice would you give?

_____

_____

_____

4.   The service manager at an auto repair shop answers the phones and schedules customers who need their cars repaired. He is responsible for scheduling each mechanic who is specially trained in different areas of auto repair work, such as vibrations, painting, collisions, and glass replacement. How would poor listening skills affect the business at this auto repair shop?

_____

_____

_____

Take a Message

When the person requested is unavailable to a caller, it is important to take a message. Unless you have an extraordinary memory, you won't remember all the messages and all the details of each. To be prepared to take messages, follow a few basic rules.

♦ Keep pen and message pads by the telephone.
♦ Write legibly.
♦ Record the message accurately.

♦ Gather sufficient information to pass along.
♦ Ask for the spelling of unusual words or names.
♦ Read the message back to the caller.

A typical phone message should include nine pieces of information. The message form in the illustration shows where information should be placed.

Put the numbers beside the correct spot on the form.

1. The name of the person called.
2. Date of the call.
3. Time of the call.
4. First and last name of the caller.
5. Firm the caller represents.
6. Caller's area code and telephone number.
7. Nature of message.
8. A clear, accurate message.
9. Your name or initials, in case questions arise regarding the call.

To **1** _____

Date **2** _____ Time **3** _____ A.M. P.M.

WHILE YOU WERE OUT

M **4** _____

Of _____ **5** _____

Phone _____ **6** _____

Area Code	Number	Extension

7

TELEPHONED		PLEASE CALL	
CALLED TO SEE YOU		WILL CALL AGAIN	
WANTS TO SEE YOU		URGENT	

| RETURNED YOUR CALL | |

Message **8** _____
_____
_____
_____
_____
_____
_____
_____
_____

Initials **9**

Now that you have the information needed from a telephone caller, what do you do with it? It does not do you, your co-worker, or your company any good if the message becomes lost or misplaced. Immediately place the message in an obvious place— on the person's desk or in a place reserved especially for telephone messages. Remember, the communication process is not complete until the message has been successfully delivered to the receiver.

Items Needed Near the Phone

If you use the telephone at work to take messages and provide information to customers or other employees, you can increase your efficiency by having a few times, in addition to pen and pad, within easy reach. Locate and keep handy the following items:

1. List of frequently phoned numbers
2. Company telephone directory
3. Company FAX number
4. Names and numbers of emergency services
5. Name and number of building services
6. Price lists if appropriate

> " If you want to understand your government, don't begin by reading the Constitution. It conveys precious little of the flavor of today's Statecraft. Instead, read selected portions of the Washington telephone directory containing listings for all the organizations with titles beginning with the word 'National'. "
>
> — George Will

Take a message

As a secretary for a estate brokerage firm, you have been asked to cover the telephone while the brokers and agents are in their monthly staff meeting. Write a message for each of the phone calls that come in during the meeting.

Call One

Michael DeVore, loan officer with First National Bank, calls at 9:45. He needs to speak to Dorothy Bankemper before the end of the day regarding the house closing scheduled for next Monday. The customer, Joe Smith, is missing vital paperwork which may cause the sale of his house to fall through. He can be reached before 3:00 at (404) 555-3540.

```
To_____
Date _____ Time _____ A.M.
                                    P.M.
        WHILE YOU WERE OUT
M _____
Of _____
Phone _____
     Area Code     Number      Extension
  ┌──────────────┬──┬──────────────┬──┐
  │ TELEPHONED   │  │ PLEASE CALL  │  │
  │ CALLED TO SEE YOU│ WILL CALL AGAIN│ │
  │ WANTS TO SEE YOU │ URGENT       │  │
  └──────────────┴──┴──────────────┴──┘
        │ RETURNED YOUR CALL │  │
Message _____
_____
_____
_____
_____
_____
_____
_____
                Initials
```

Call Two

Hosny Hamia calls at 10:12. He has a lunch meeting with John Worth scheduled for today. He has car trouble and will be late for lunch. Although the problem is minor, he will be about 45 minutes late. He plans to still meet John at the restaurant, unless John wants to reschedule the meeting for another day. His cell phone number is (771) 555-1996. He is at Drake's Auto Shop at (771) 555-2173.

Call Three

A prospective client, Holly Freewynn, calls long distance to speak to the agent Sandi Copeland. Holly is relocating to your city and wants information on the suburbs in the city. She needs information on schools in the area, property taxes, and other community resources by 4:30 today. She is flying in tomorrow and wants to schedule time with Sandi. She will only be in town for 2 days. She can be reached at home at (513) 555-4210 or you can page her at (513) 555-3108.

| To_____ |
| Date _____ Time _____ A.M. P.M. |

WHILE YOU WERE OUT

M _____

Of _____

Phone _____

Area Code   Number   Extension

TELEPHONED		PLEASE CALL	
CALLED TO SEE YOU		WILL CALL AGAIN	
WANTS TO SEE YOU		URGENT	
RETURNED YOUR CALL		

Message _____
_____
_____
_____
_____
_____
_____
_____

Initials

| To_____ |
| Date _____ Time _____ A.M. P.M. |

WHILE YOU WERE OUT

M _____

Of _____

Phone _____

Area Code   Number   Extension

TELEPHONED		PLEASE CALL	
CALLED TO SEE YOU		WILL CALL AGAIN	
WANTS TO SEE YOU		URGENT	
RETURNED YOUR CALL		

Message _____
_____
_____
_____
_____
_____
_____
_____

Initials

Are Others Listening?

When you listen to a radio talk show, you receive a message from the announcer that goes beyond spoken words. The announcer may communicate anger, sadness, surprise, shock, disappointment. or joy. The person's inflections, volume, and vocabulary contributes to the message being conveyed. Even though you cannot see the announcer talking, the person's voice reflects mood or feelings.

When you talk on the phone, your mood affects tone of voice. A cheerful, bad, or sad mood travels through the telephone, so even if you are sick, tired, worried, or stressed, keep your voice warm, positive, and courteous. Employers, business callers, and customers expect you to be cheerful and pleasant, regardless of your mood.

The following tips can help you create a positive telephone image:

1. Be warm and pleasant.
2. Make your voice smile.
3. Use a natural tone.
4. Avoid a monotone.
5. Be alert and interested.
6. Use a normal volume.
7. Speak at a moderate rate.

You should also pronounce words properly, enunciate distinctly, avoid speaking rapidly, and use appropriate vocabulary.

Pronounce words properly

Learn the correct pronunciations of words and then practice what you've learned. Consult the dictionary or, better yet, locate CD-ROM's and on-line dictionaries that provide the pronunciation of words.

Enunciate distinctly

A mumbled message frustrates callers. Even if you can say the words correctly, if you mumble, no one will ever hear you. Use a clear, distinct voice to get your message across.

Talk at a moderate speed

You may have a lot of information to convey in a short period of time, but speaking too fast is counterproductive to your telephone listener. The listener may feel rushed, anxious, and insulted. On the other hand, speaking too slowly sends a message that you lack energy and enthusiasm. Your best bet is to speak at a moderate rate.

Use appropriate language

Save slang language for your friends. When you are at work, express yourself in a professional manner. Avoid using foul language, technical terms, and derogatory statements. Keep your language appropriate for the situation.

ACTIVITY 8.4

A Voice Self-Assessment

What message does your voice convey? Complete the self-assessment below to learn more about the hidden messages in your voice.

1. People often ask me many questions during a telephone call because I speak too fast and they don't get all the information.   Always   Sometimes   Never

2. I only mumble when I'm in a bad mood or feeling very tired at work.   Always   Sometimes   Never

3. When I call co-workers, I speak to them like they are my personal friends.   Always   Sometimes   Never

4. When I have difficulty pronouncing a word, I just say "You know what I mean."   Always   Sometimes   Never

5. My voice is hoarse and raspy in the morning when I first get to work.   Always   Sometimes   Never

6. I talk softly when I am on the phone because I don't want my supervisor to overhear any of my conversations.   Always   Sometimes   Never

7. I do not slow down when I give phone numbers or addresses out over the phone. I assume the caller will ask me to repeat if they don't understand.   Always   Sometimes   Never

8. I use technical terms when I speak to customers so I can learn how much they know about our product.   Always   Sometimes   Never

9. I use a monotone voice so the caller cannot distinguish my mood.   Always   Sometimes   Never

10. I usually slouch, lean back and relax when I'm on the phone since the caller can't see what I'm doing.   Always   Sometimes   Never

If you answered "always" or "sometimes" to any of the questions above, your voice may not be conveying the right message. Your voice qualities leave a lasting impression of yourself and your company.

GETTING CONNECTED

For more information on the message your voice sends, log on to the Internet and explore the World Wide Web site Telephone Skills at:

http://www.changedynamics.com/samples/telephon.htm

WORKSHOP WRAP-UP

- The telephone is an important business tool.
- Telephone conversations deserve your attention.
- Listening on the telephone involves concentration, listening for main ideas, asking questions, and repeating information for clarity.
- Don't rely on your memory. Write down telephone messages.
- Your voice leaves an impression on each caller.

Checklist for Listening and Observing

✓ Know that listening is a process.

✓ Learn to sense, interpret, and evaluate what you hear.

✓ Use all your senses to be a smart listener.

✓ Recognize that more time is spent listening than any other form of communication.

✓ Understand that only a small amount of time is spent on listening training.

✓ Know that most people listen carefully only 25 percent of the time.

✓ Use feedback to clarify the message.

✓ Refrain from interrupting the speaker with questions.

✓ Refrain from talking when you should be listening

✓ Avoid planning what you are going to say while you are supposed to be listening.

✓ Refrain from putting words in the speaker's mouth.

✓ Make eye contact with the speaker.

✓ Tune out distractions.

✓ Ask questions for clarity.

✓ Recognize that different situations require different types of listening.

✓ Try to learn something new from listening

✓ Show concern when you listen.

✓ Build relationships through active listening.

✓ Be a courteous listener.

✓ Engage in empathetic, critical, and appreciative listening.

✓ Passive listening is the least effective.

✓ Be alert to key works or phrases when you listen.

✓ Refrain from judging the speaker.

✓ Focus on the content of the message.

✓ Listen with intensity.

✓ Listen to the mood and demeanor of the speaker.

✓ Refrain from trying to fix the speaker's problem.

✓ Clarify messages by asking questions.

✓ Distractions in the environment can interfere with listening.

✓ Be aware of distractions you encounter in listening situations.

✓ Listening barriers can be external or internal.

Checklist for Listening and Observing continued

✓ Search for internal listening barriers.

✓ Learn to control internal barriers to listening.

✓ Recognize when static enters the listening process.

✓ Identify the source of listening static.

✓ Control listening static whenever possible.

✓ Remove talking as a listening barrier.

✓ Avoid becoming the listening barrier when you are the speaker.

✓ Value listening as well as talking.

✓ Make up your mind to listen.

✓ Maintain eye contact with the speaker.

✓ Mentally paraphrase what is being said.

✓ Pay close attention to non-verbal clues.

✓ Use facial expressions for feedback.

✓ Uncross arms to reduce negative feedback.

✓ Listen to the whole message, verbal and non-verbal.

✓ Recognize listening filters.

✓ Understand the listening filters of those around you.

✓ Ask specific, not general, questions.

✓ Keep questions on the topic.

✓ Ask for explanations and definitions.

✓ Recognize that timing is everything.

✓ Listen for the main idea in telephone conversations.

✓ Pronounce words proper and enunciate distinctly during telephone conversations.

Listening Tips

Levels of Listening

Listening Level	What's Heard	Needed for Next
First level	Basic, but incomplete, information *"The copier is not working"*	Who and what details
Second level	A limited amount of important information	Additional details, accurate details
Third level	Most, but not all, of the important information	Details that give the full story
Fourth level	All important information heard, but limited supporting details heard	Correct supporting information plus interpretation of message from behaviors and tone of the speaker
Fifth level	All important and supporting information "The copier technician was here. She needs a part and will be back Thursday to finish the job. We should not use the copier except in an emergency even though the machine will now make copies. I think she was playing it safe when she said not to make copies. She said that the part was a minor one that is worn but not heavily damaged."	